Tips for Being
Organised
Like a Boss!

And Motivating Quotes

Tips for Being Organised Like a Boss!
And Motivating Quotes

Copyright © 2020 by Rachel Townsend –
Secretarial Online

ISBN: 978 1 716 33406 1
First Printing: 2020
Secretarial Online
Penrith, NSW 2750
www.secretarialonline.com.au

Cover and internal designed by Domenika Fairy
Email: dfairy@internode.on.net

Australian trade bookstores and wholesalers:
Please contact Secretarial Online
Tel: 0414 784 428 or
email rachel@secretarialonline.com.au

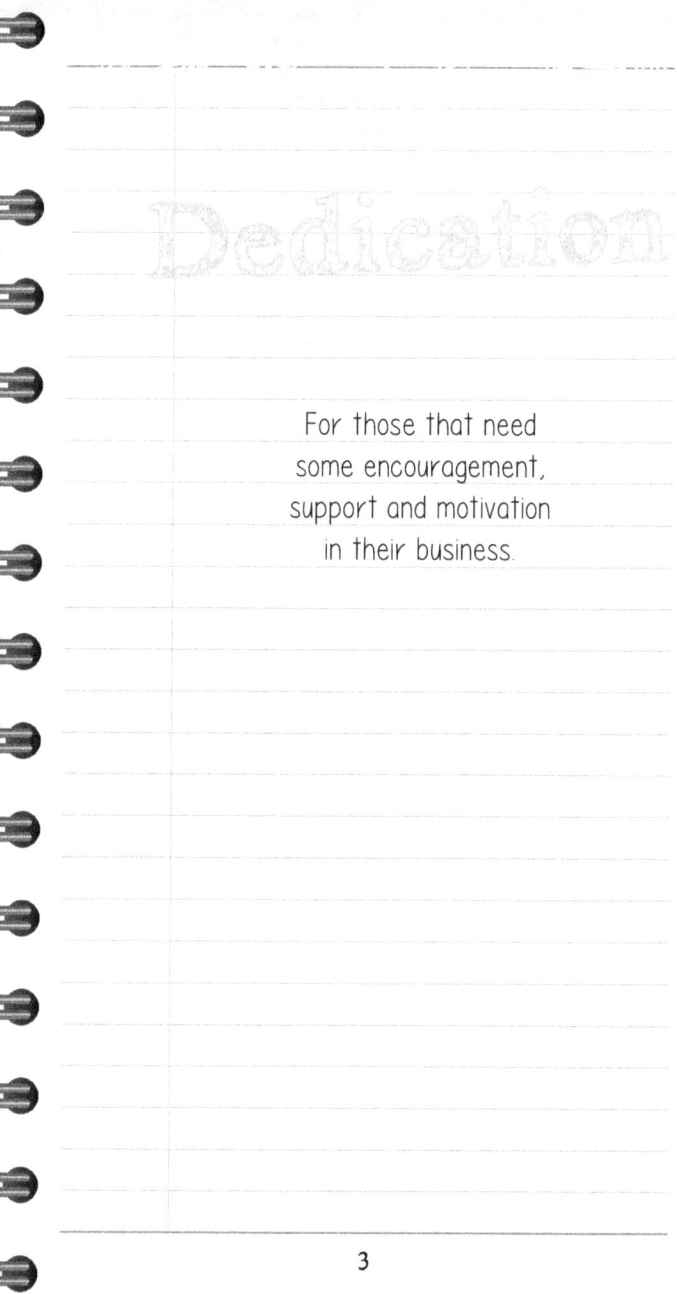

Dedication

For those that need
some encouragement,
support and motivation
in their business.

Quote

Rome wasn't built in a day.
With hard work and
perseverance
it will get better

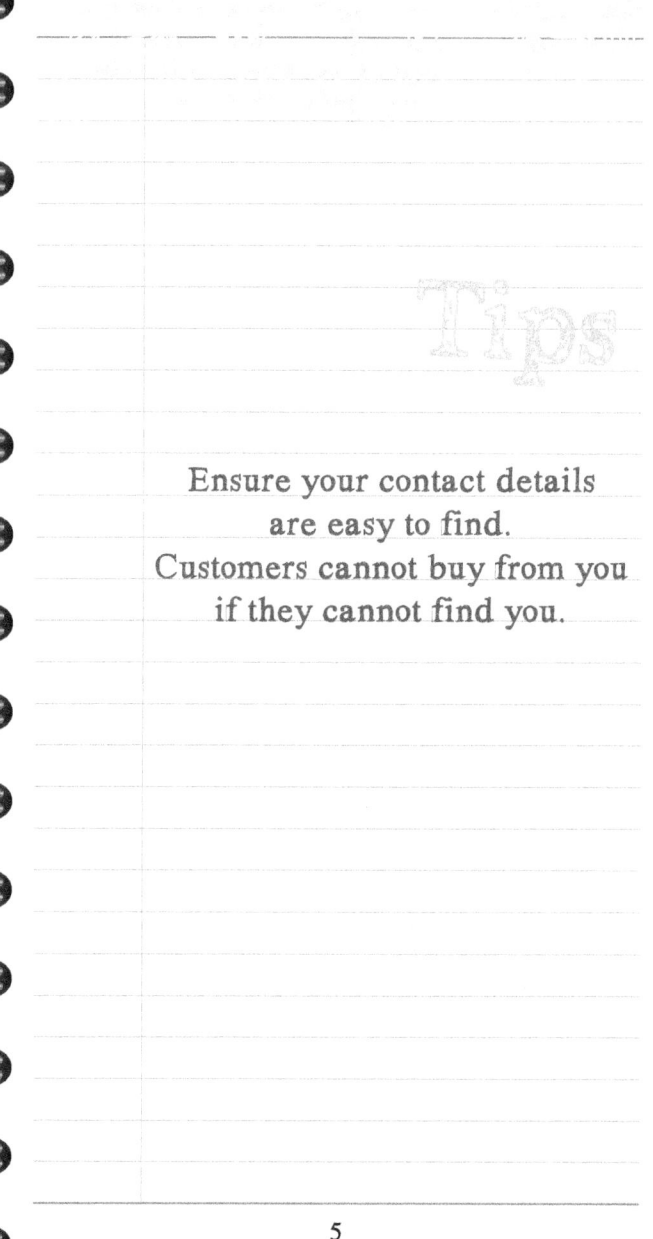

Tips

Ensure your contact details
are easy to find.
Customers cannot buy from you
if they cannot find you.

Quote

Nothing will work
unless you do
MAYA ANGELOU

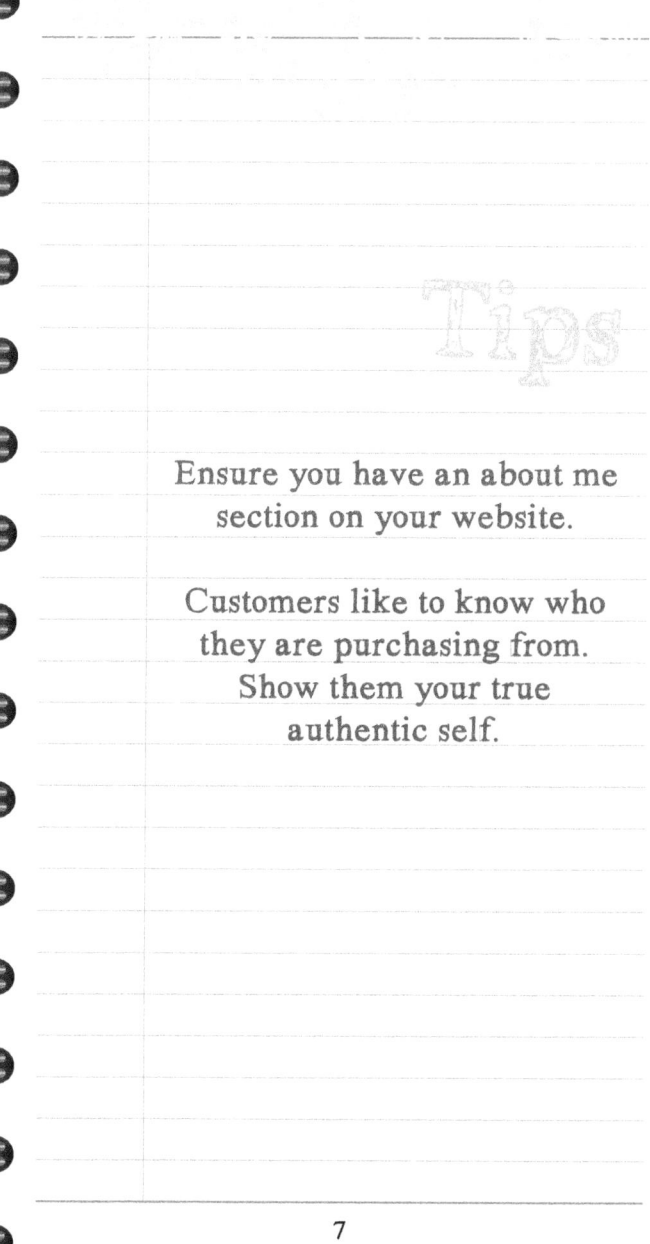

Tips

Ensure you have an about me section on your website.

Customers like to know who they are purchasing from. Show them your true authentic self.

Quote

We can't help everyone,
but everyone can help someone
RONALD REAGAN

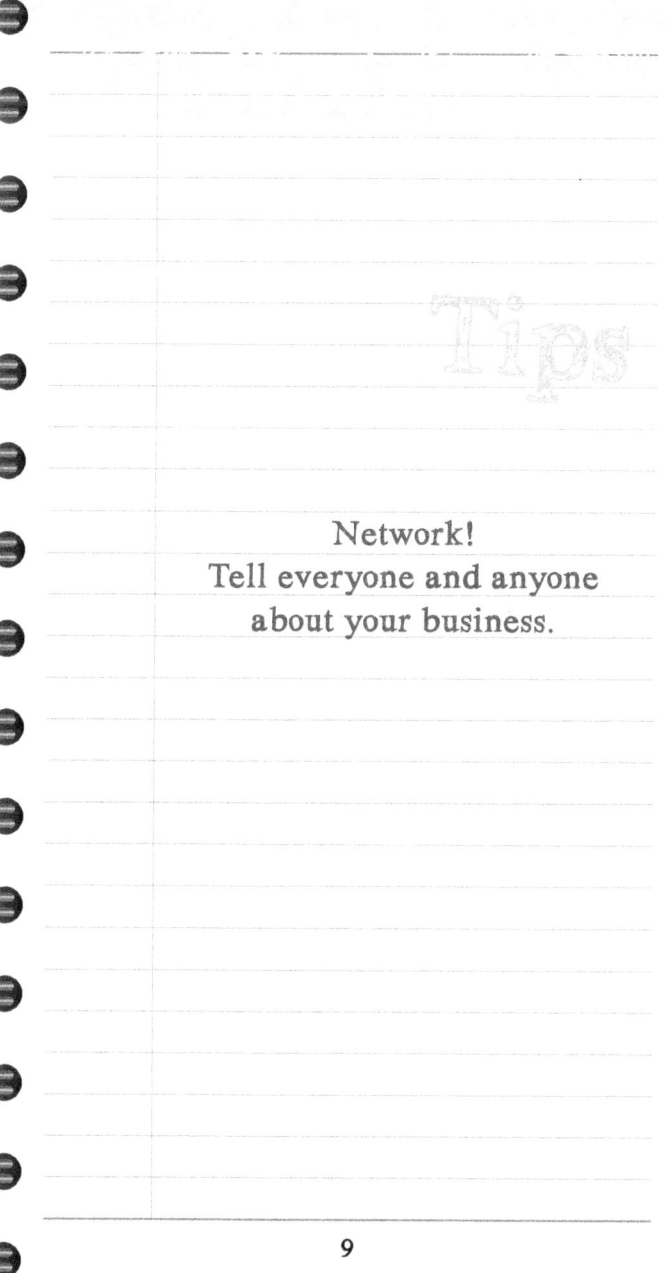

Tips

Network!
Tell everyone and anyone
about your business.

Quote

Everything you've ever wanted
is on the other side of fear

GEORGE ADDAIR

Tips

Be organized.
Plan your week!

Quote

The future depends
on what you do today
MAHATMA GHANDI

Tips

Set boundaries -
it is ok to not check
your phone 24/7

Quote

The only way to do great work,
is to love what you do

STEVE JOBS

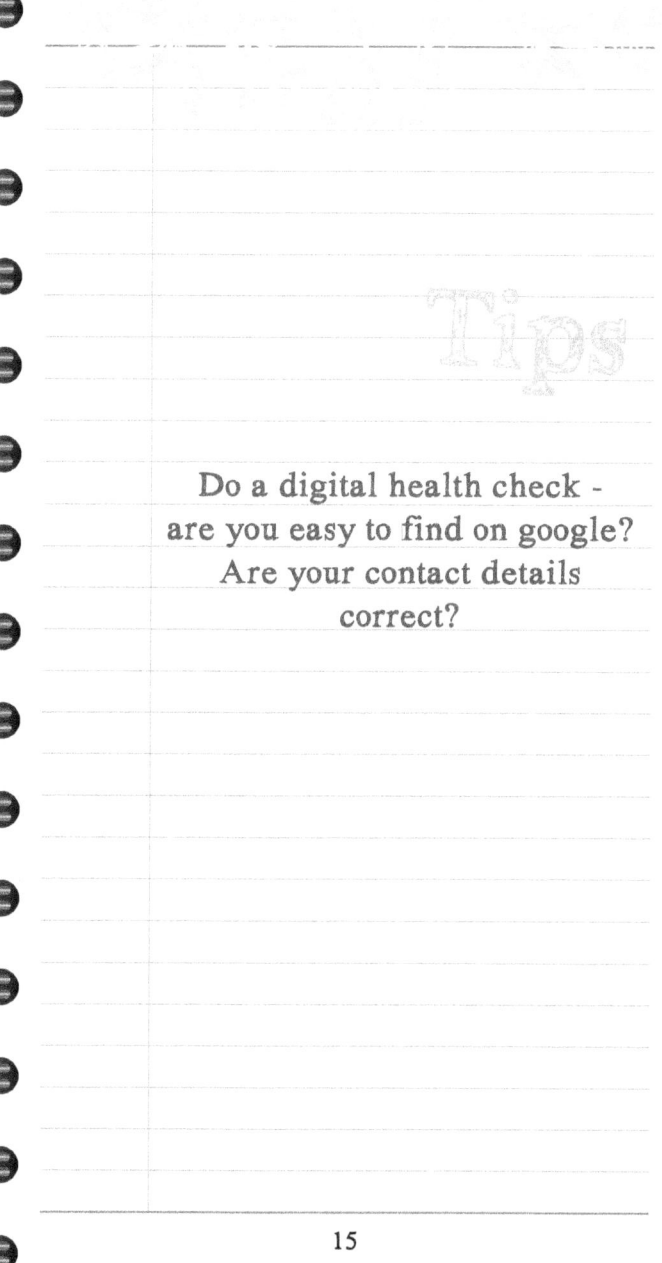

Tips

Do a digital health check -
are you easy to find on google?
Are your contact details
correct?

Quote

Strive not to be a success,
but rather to be of value.

ALBERT EINSTEIN

Tips

Provide great customer service -
answer all email and
phone enquiries.

Quote

Either you run the day,
or the day runs you

JIM ROHN

Tips

Research your target market -
provide a service
that your customers need.

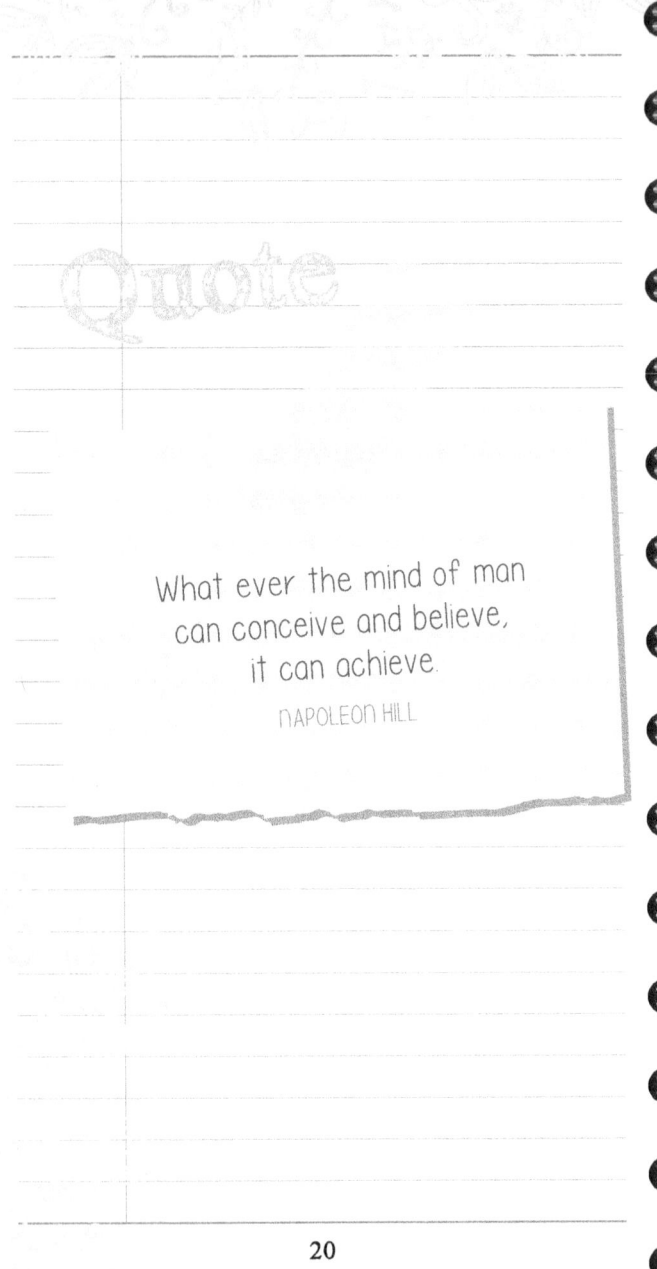

Quote

What ever the mind of man
can conceive and believe,
it can achieve.

NAPOLEON HILL

Tips

Work hard -
nothing will work unless
you put time and effort in.

Quote

If you can dream it,
you can do it
WALT DISNEY

Tips

Continue to learn and
expand your knowledge.

Quote

Build your own dreams,
or someone else will hire you
to build theirs

FARRAH GRAY

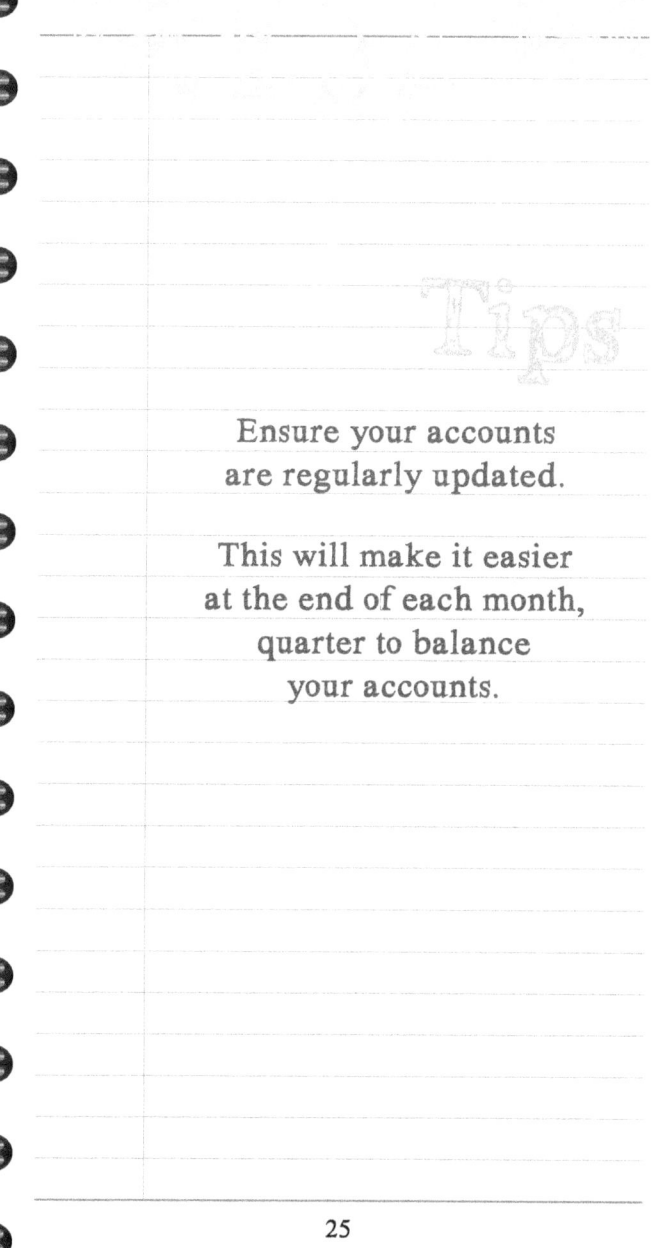

Tips

Ensure your accounts
are regularly updated.

This will make it easier
at the end of each month,
quarter to balance
your accounts.

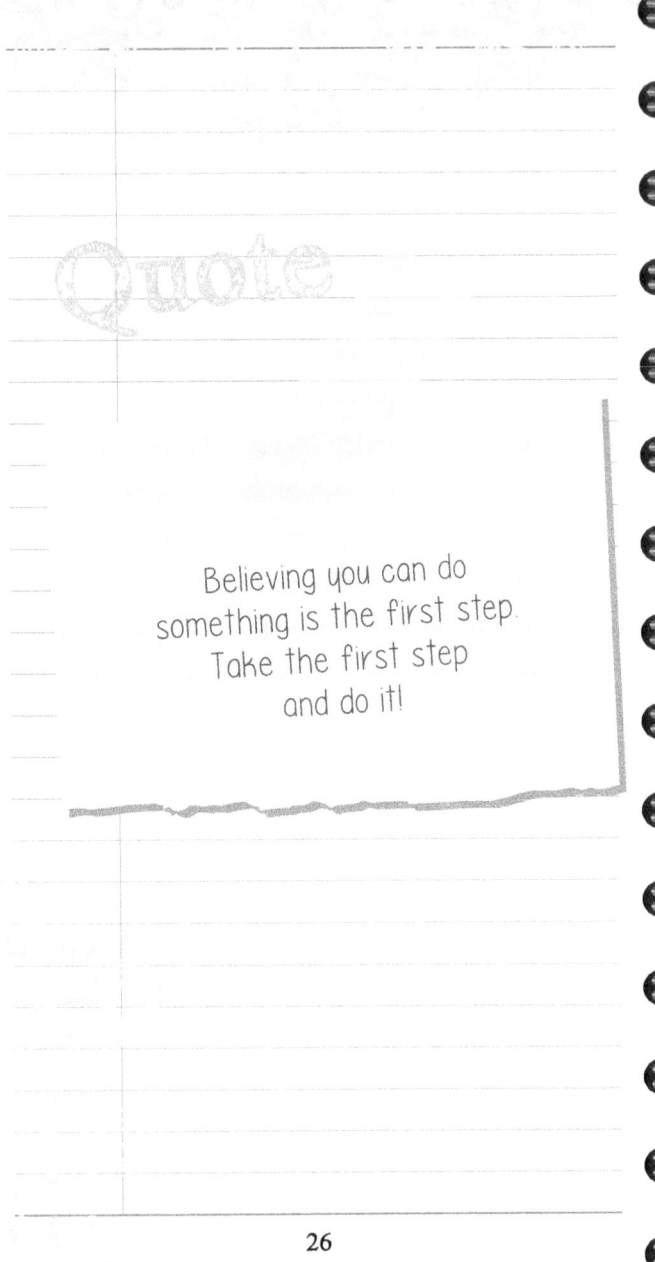

Quote

Believing you can do
something is the first step.
Take the first step
and do it!

Tips

Support your local community
and they in turn
will support you.

Quote

Time is more valuable
than money.
You can always get
more money, but you cannot
get more time.

JIM ROHN

Tips

Start a blog -
share your knowledge
and expertise.

Doing this regularly helps
your customers build trust and
then will go to you first when
they need information.

If you improve 1% each day,
within a year,
you will have improved 365%.
Think about that!

unknown

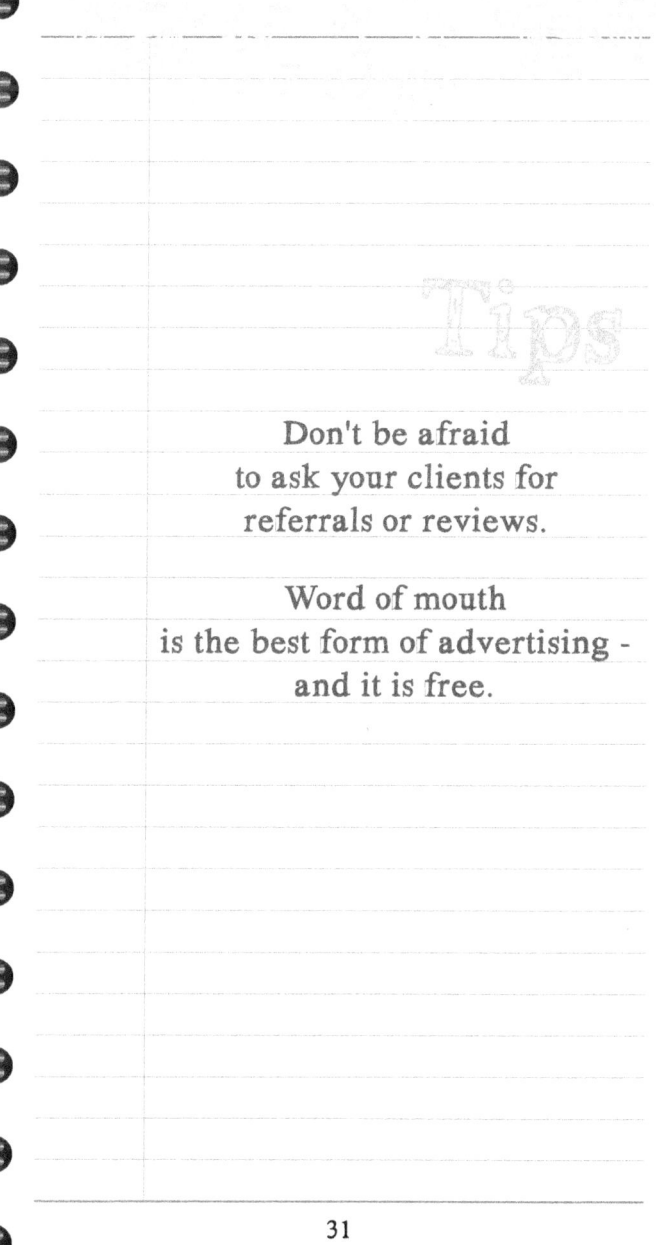

Tips

Don't be afraid
to ask your clients for
referrals or reviews.

Word of mouth
is the best form of advertising -
and it is free.

Quote

Believe you can,
and you are halfway there.
THEODORE ROOSEVELT

Tips

Find your niche -
do what you have expertise in.

Focus on the things you do well
for your customers.
It is best to do something
that you are good at
rather than offer extra services
where you are not so good at.

Quote

Success is liking yourself,
liking what you do,
and liking how you do it

MAYA ANGELOU

Tips

Use apps and programs
to streamline your business.

There are lots of
time saving apps which can
assist you to manage,
delegate and complete
your work.

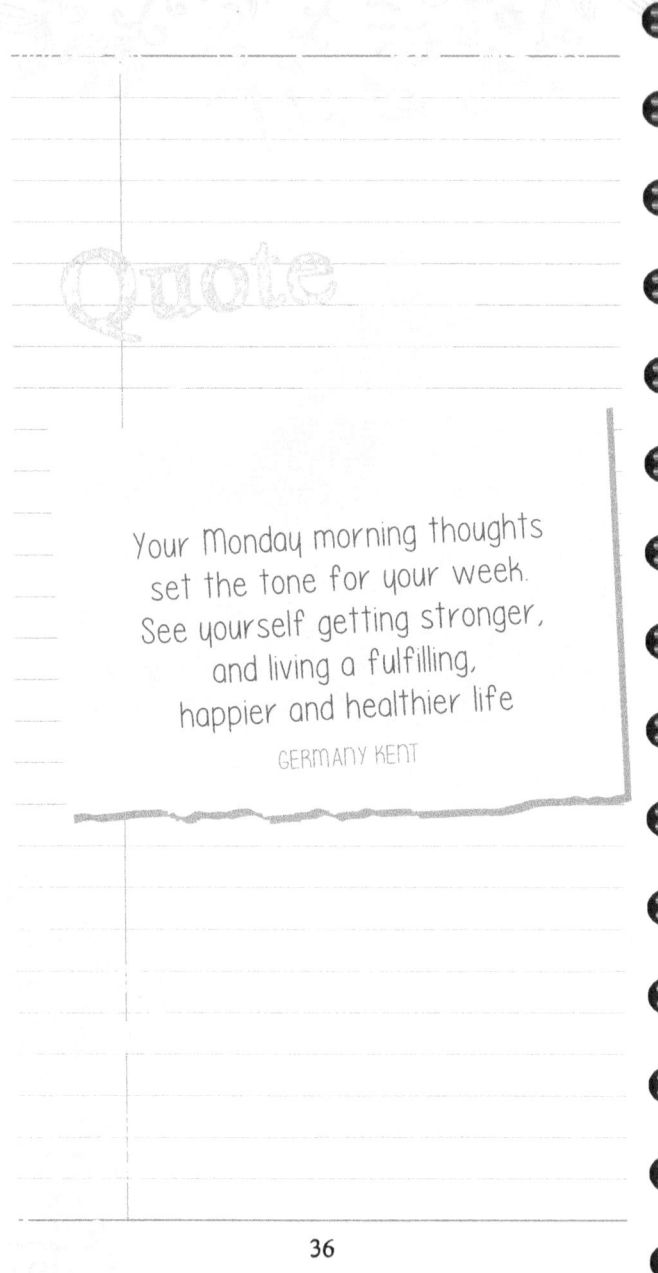

Quote

Your Monday morning thoughts
set the tone for your week.
See yourself getting stronger,
and living a fulfilling,
happier and healthier life

GERMANY KENT

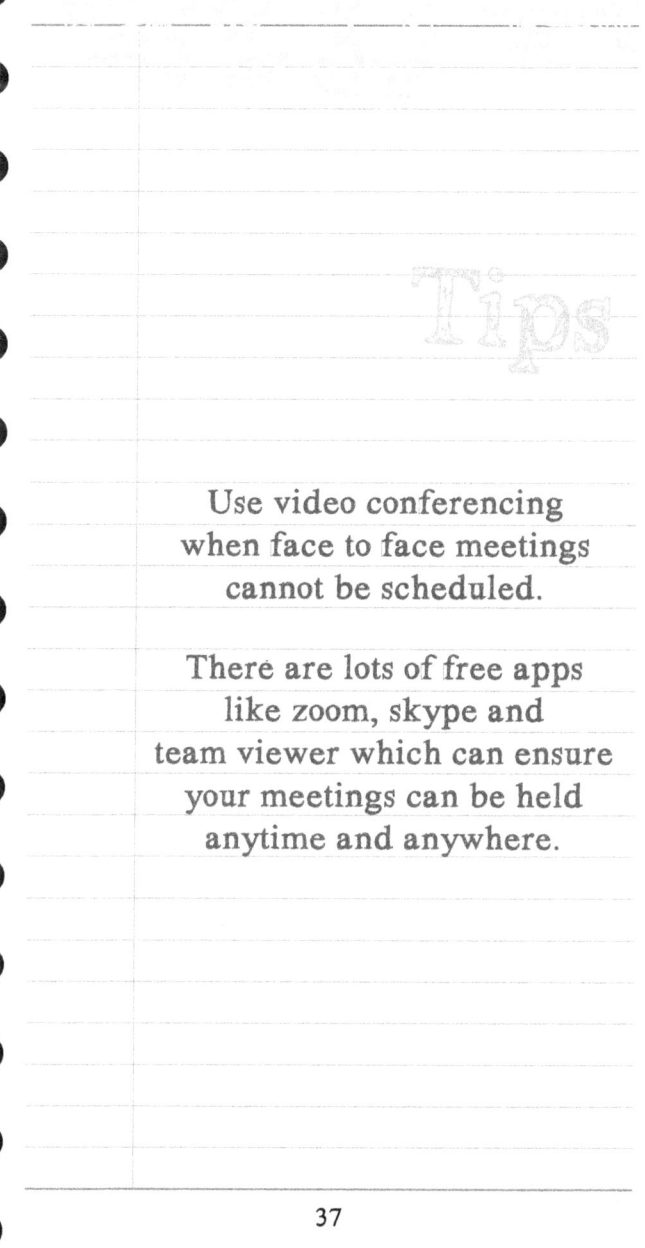

Tips

Use video conferencing
when face to face meetings
cannot be scheduled.

There are lots of free apps
like zoom, skype and
team viewer which can ensure
your meetings can be held
anytime and anywhere.

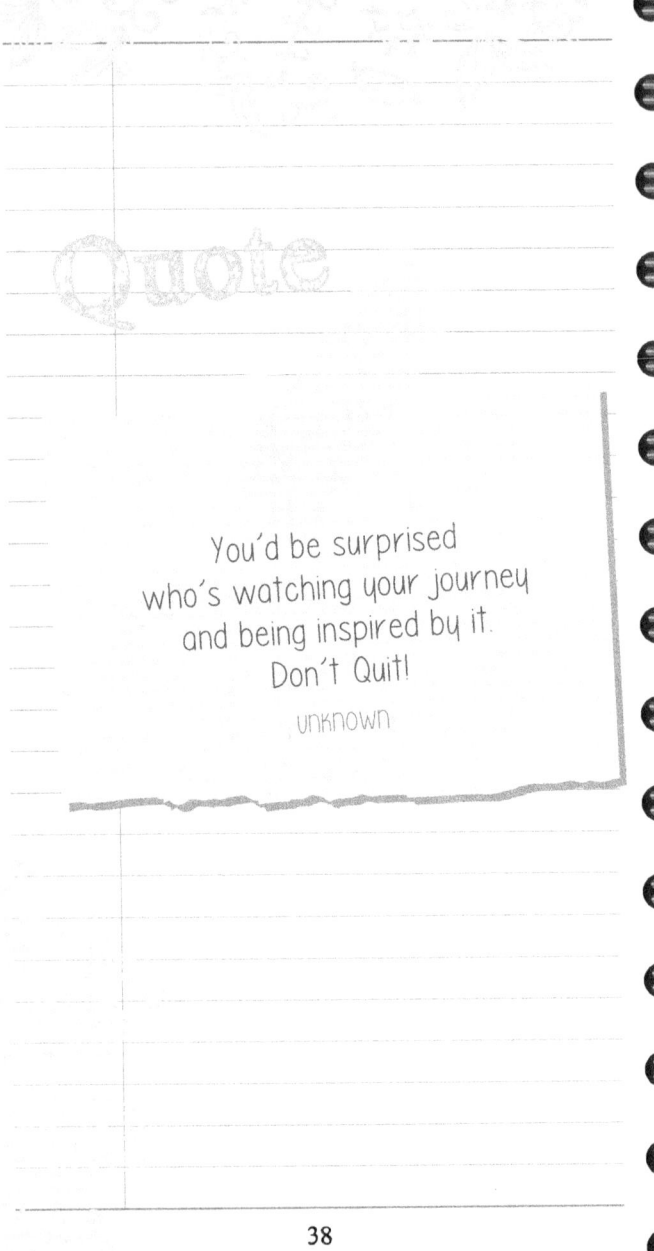

Quote

You'd be surprised
who's watching your journey
and being inspired by it.
Don't Quit!

unknown

38

Tips

Use project management apps
to communicate with staff,
manage tasks and deadlines.

Quote

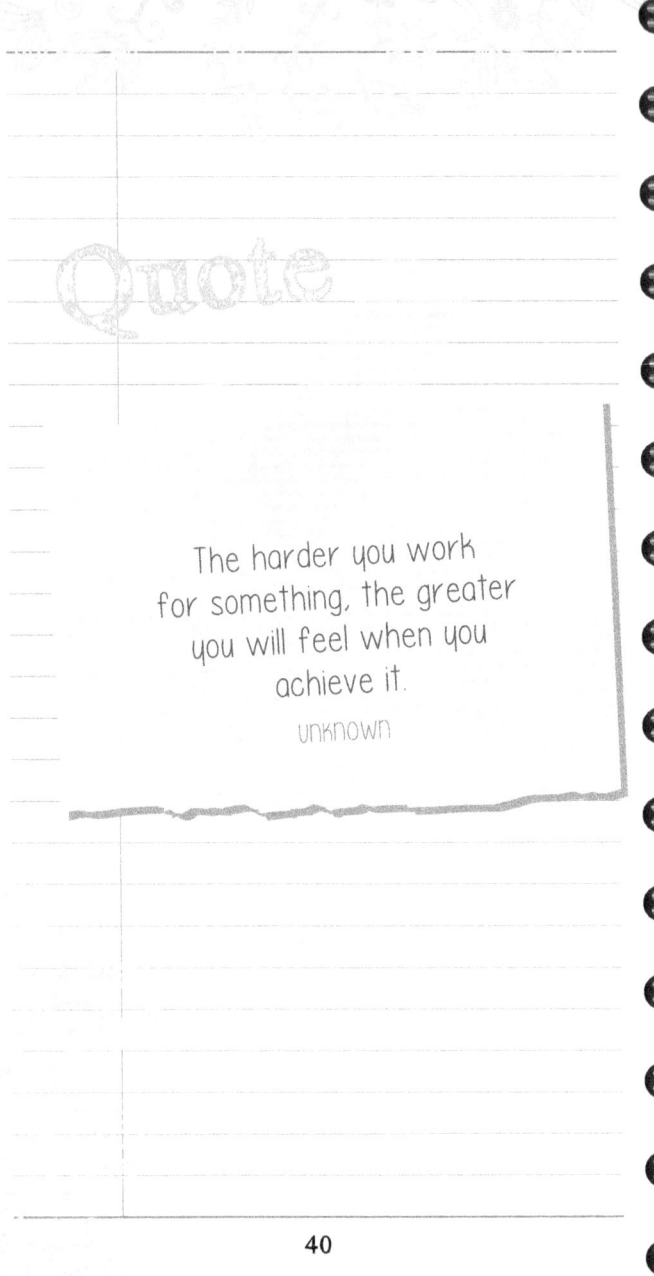

The harder you work
for something, the greater
you will feel when you
achieve it.

Unknown

Tips

Use messaging apps
to communicate with your team
in real time.

Quote

Do something today
that your future will
thank you for

unknown

Tips

Delegate tasks
to save you time.

Utilise the
skills and abilities
of those around you.

Quote

Opportunities don't happen,
you create them.
CHRIS GROSSER

Tips

Use social media -
everyone is on it,
make sure your business
is seen!

Quote

To accomplish great things, we
must not only act,
but also dream, not only plan,
but also believe

ANATOLE FRANCE

Tips

Don't compare yourself
to others. Your business,
your business journey.

Quote

We are what we repeatedly do.
Excellence, then is not an act,
but a habit.

ARISTOTLE

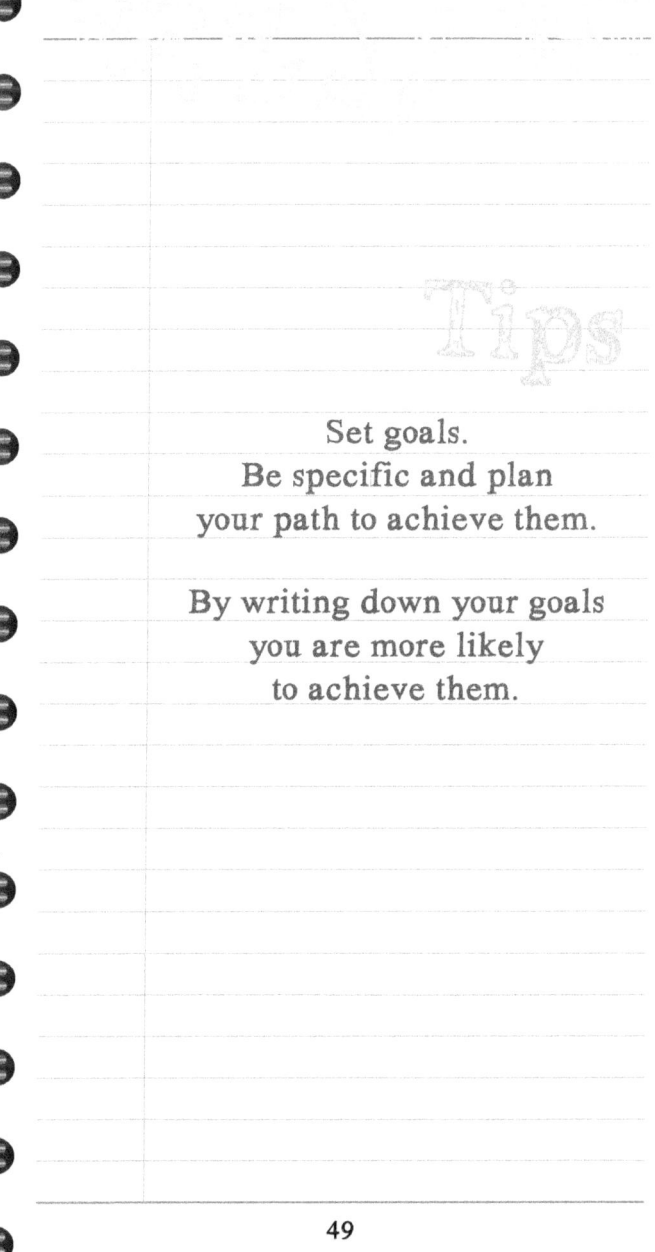

Tips

Set goals.
Be specific and plan
your path to achieve them.

By writing down your goals
you are more likely
to achieve them.

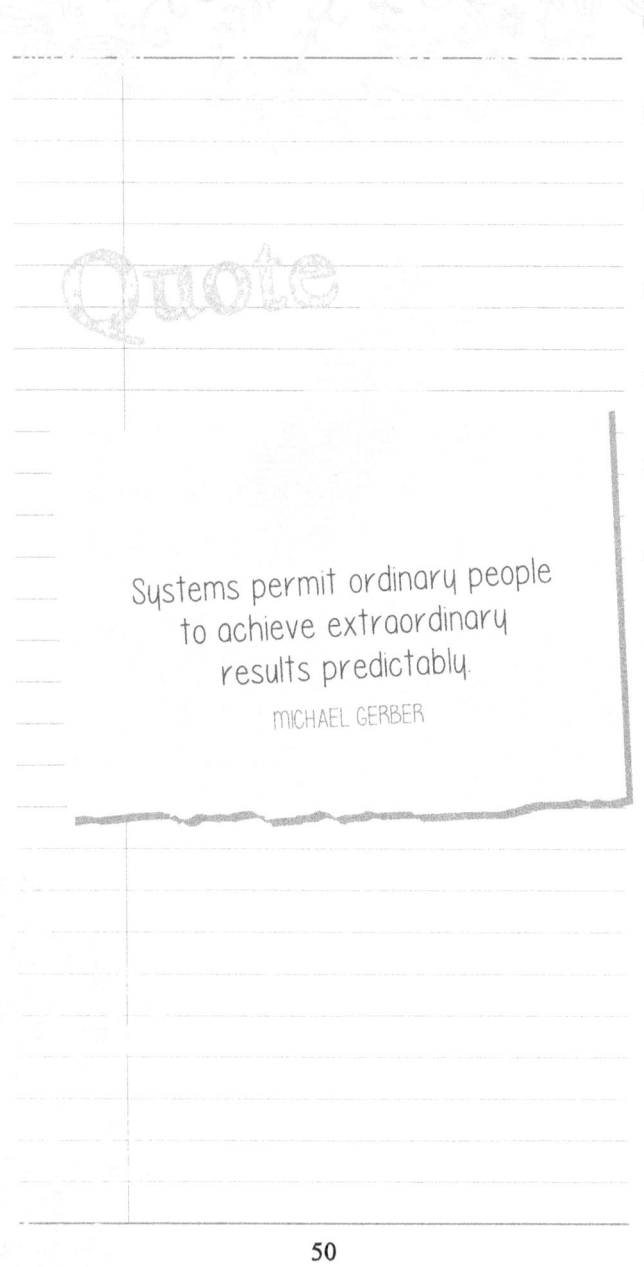

Quote

Systems permit ordinary people
to achieve extraordinary
results predictably.

MICHAEL GERBER

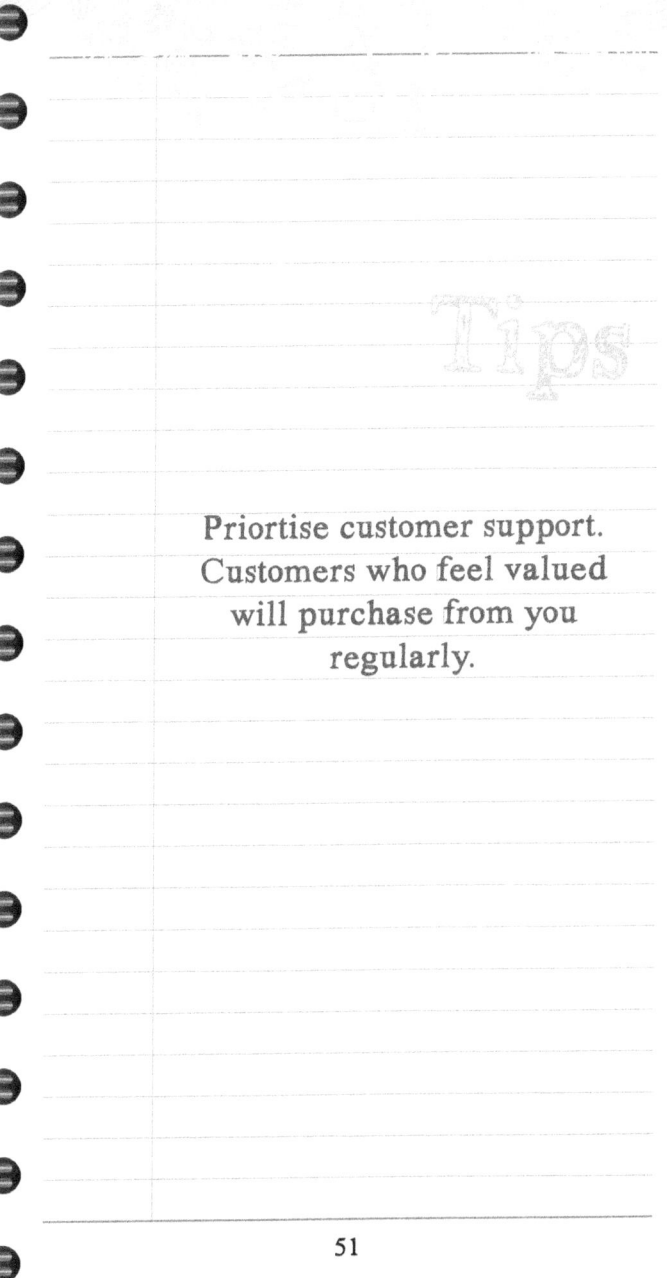

Tips

Priortise customer support.
Customers who feel valued
will purchase from you
regularly.

Quote

Success usually comes
to those are too busy
to look for it
.
HENRY DAVID THOREAU

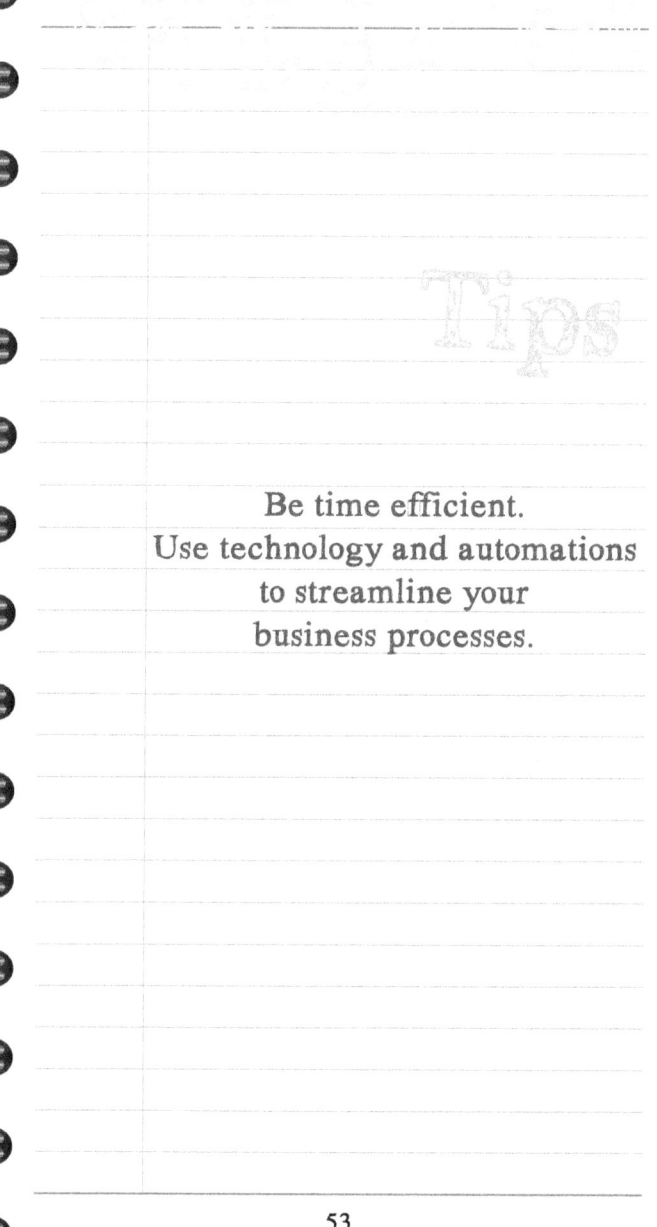

Tips

Be time efficient.
Use technology and automations
to streamline your
business processes.

Quote

Success usually
comes to those who are
too busy to look for it

HENRY DAVID THOREAU

Tips

Use social media
to advertise your business
at little or no cost.

Quote

The ones who are
crazy enough to think
they can change the world,
are the ones that do.

unknown

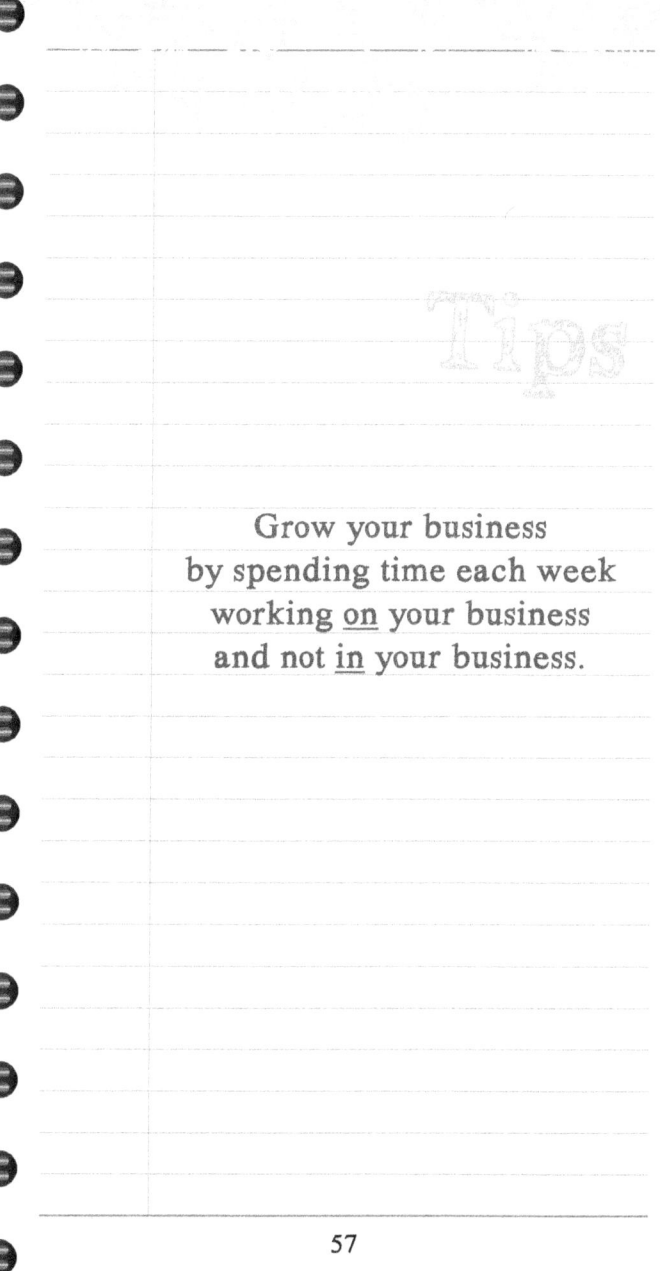

Tips

Grow your business
by spending time each week
working <u>on</u> your business
and not <u>in</u> your business.

Quote

Don't let the fear of losing
be greater than the
excitement of winning

ROBERT KIYOSAKI

Tips

Keep detailed records -
this will allow you to know
where your business stands
financially.

Quote

There are no secrets
to success. It is the result
of preparation, hard work and,
learning from failure,

COLIN POWELL

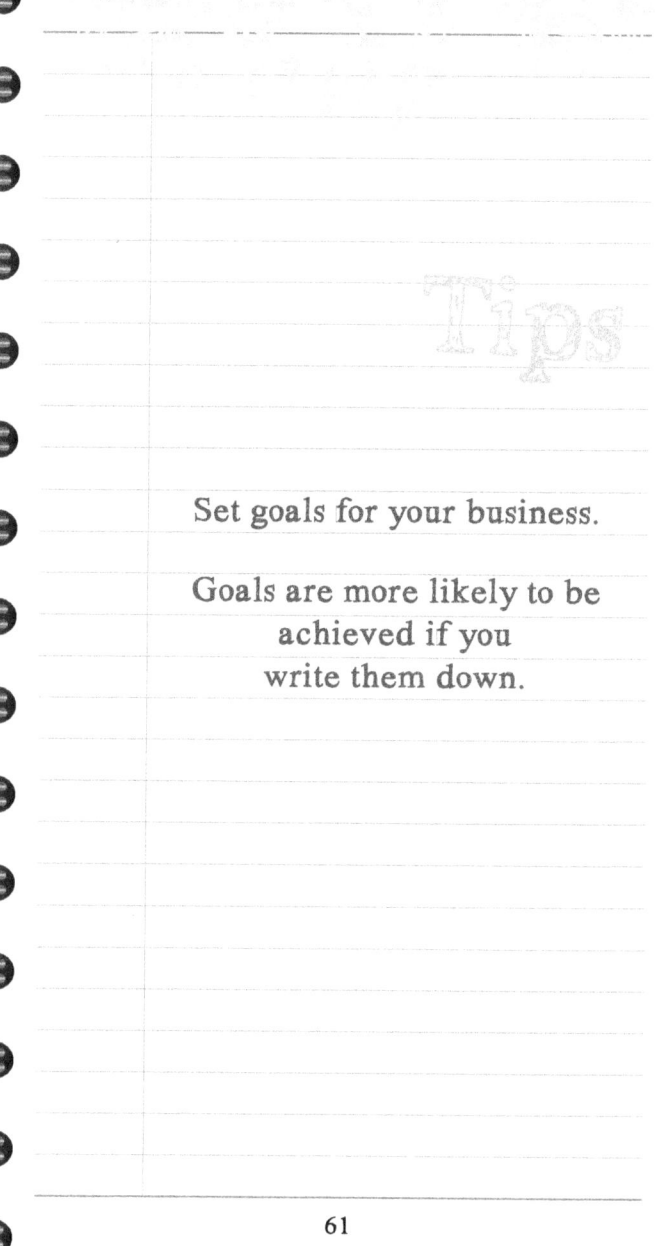

Tips

Set goals for your business.

Goals are more likely to be
achieved if you
write them down.

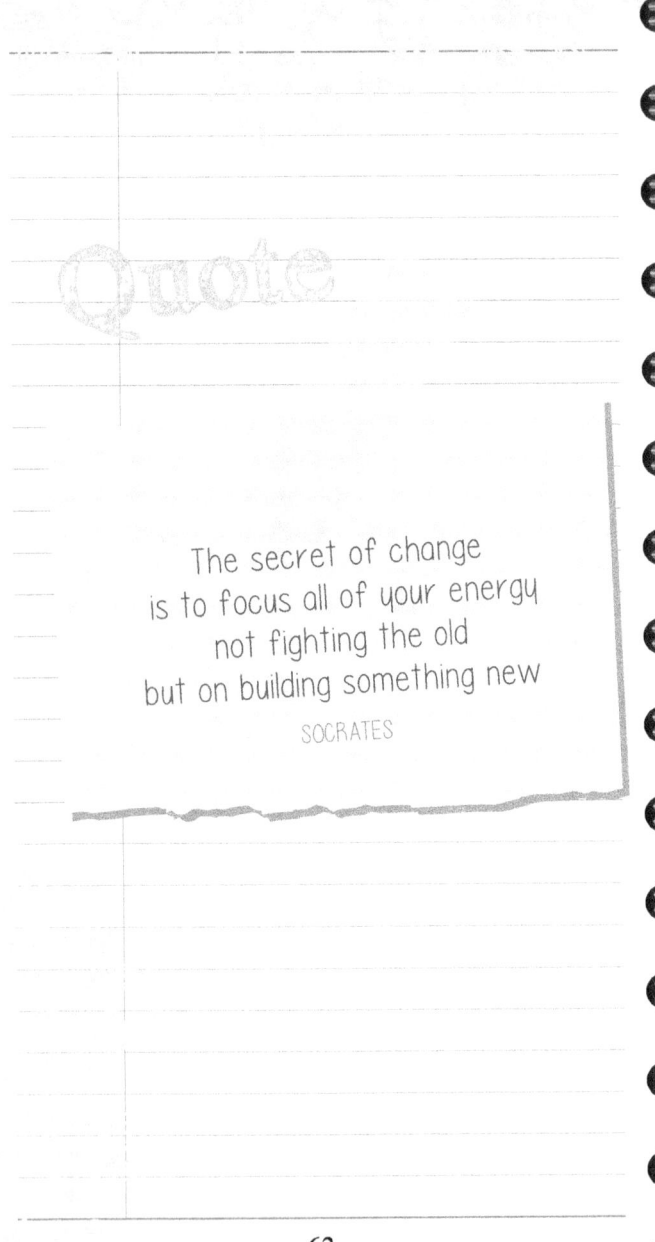

Quote

The secret of change
is to focus all of your energy
not fighting the old
but on building something new

SOCRATES

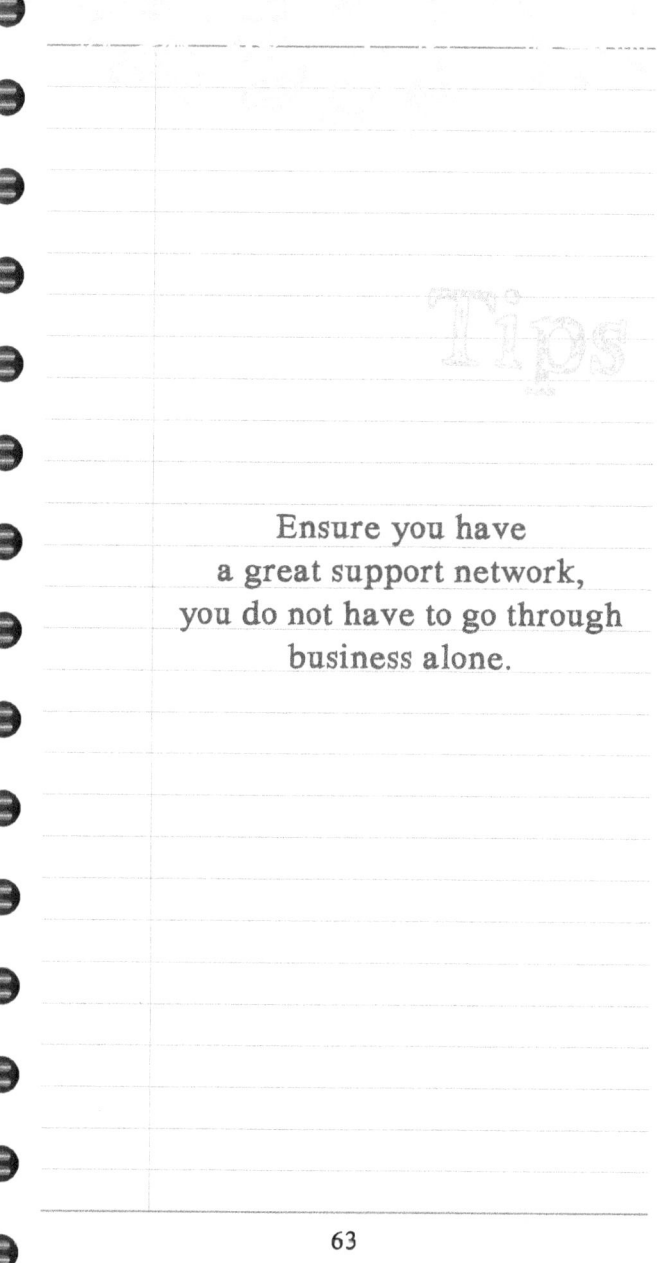

Tips

Ensure you have
a great support network,
you do not have to go through
business alone.

Your most unhappy customers
are your greatest source
of learning

BILL GATES

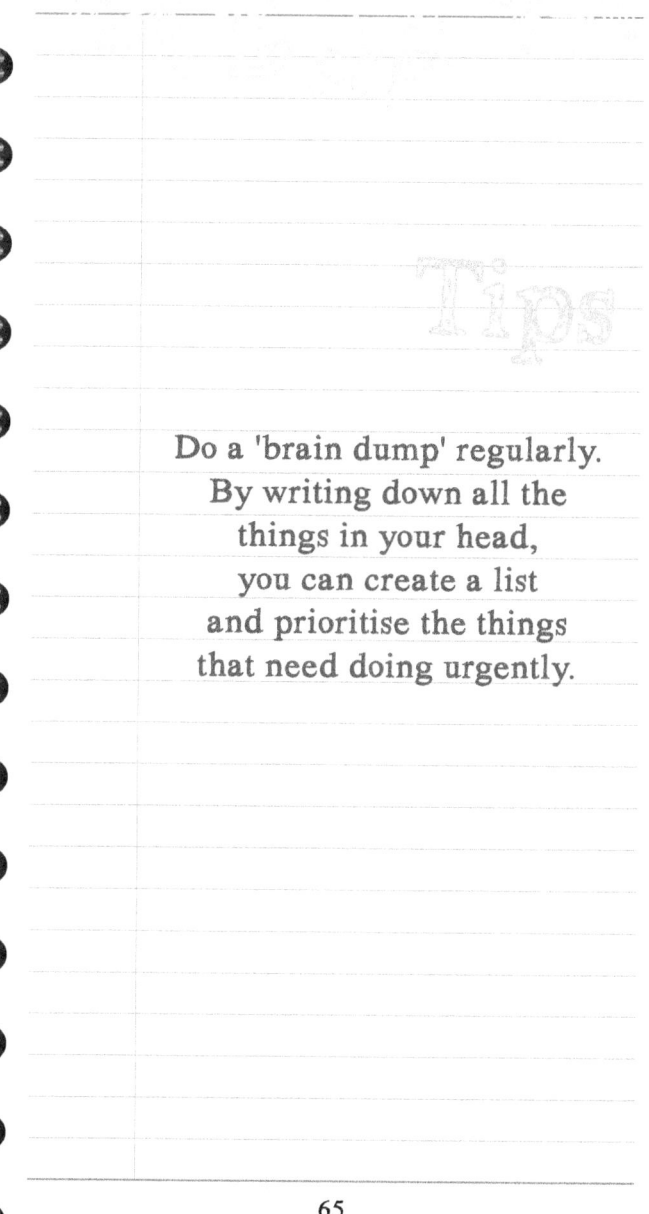

Tips

Do a 'brain dump' regularly.
By writing down all the
things in your head,
you can create a list
and prioritise the things
that need doing urgently.

Quote

Make the most of yourself
by fanning the tiny,
inner sparks of possibility
into flames of achievement

GOLDA MEIR

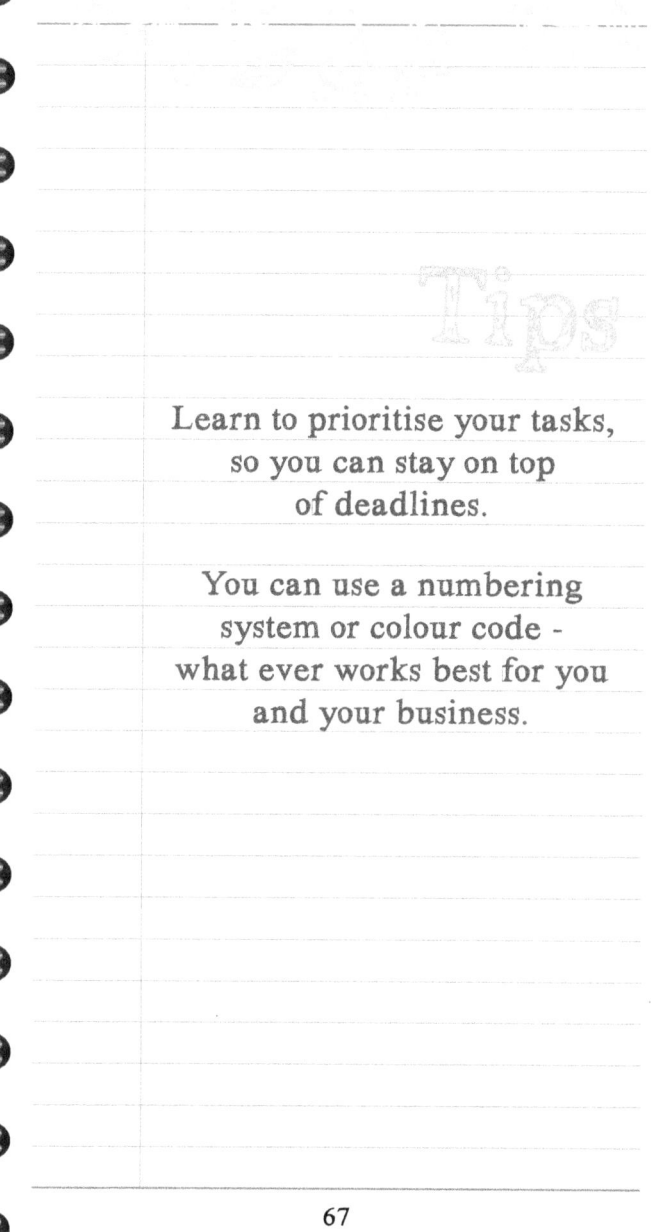

Tips

Learn to prioritise your tasks,
so you can stay on top
of deadlines.

You can use a numbering
system or colour code -
what ever works best for you
and your business.

Quote

The fastest way
to change yourself is to
hang out with people
who are already the way
you want to be

REID HOFFMAN

Use a 'vision board'
to help you visualize your goals
and plans for your business.

It doesn't have to be
anything fancy -
just a pin board with
pictures and text of
what you want to achieve
in your business and ideas
you want to explore.

Quote

Chase the vision,
not the money, the money
will end up following you

TOY HSIEH

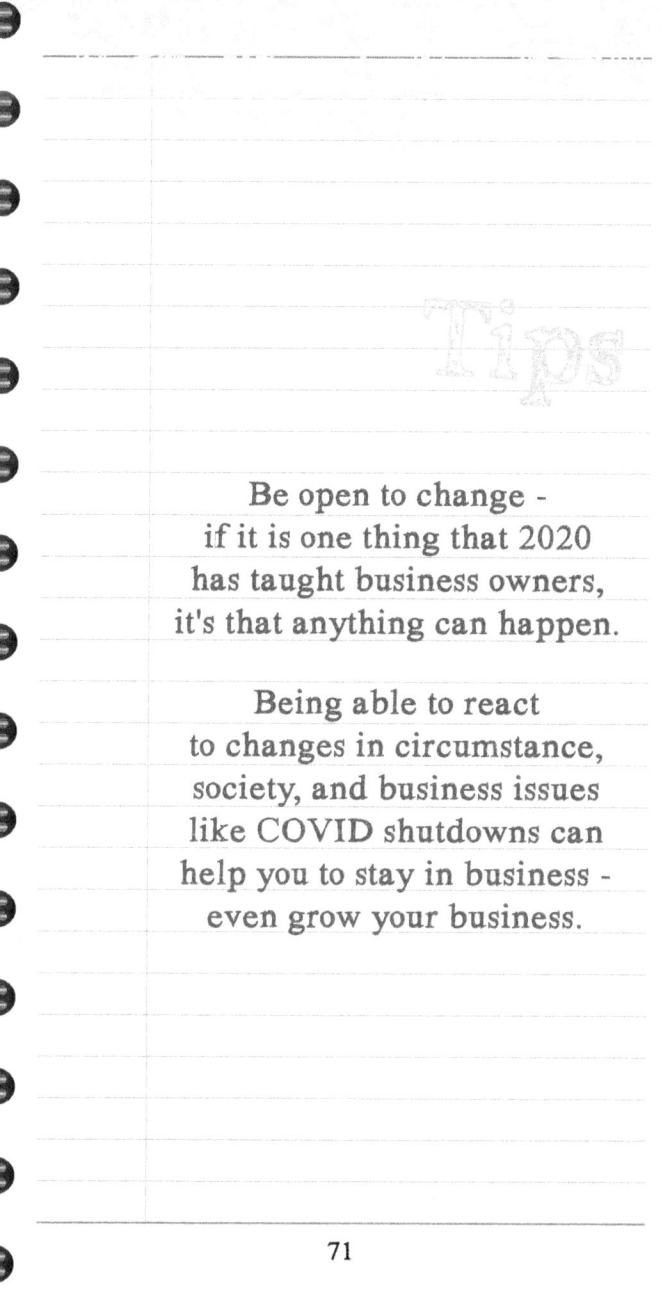

Tips

Be open to change -
if it is one thing that 2020
has taught business owners,
it's that anything can happen.

Being able to react
to changes in circumstance,
society, and business issues
like COVID shutdowns can
help you to stay in business -
even grow your business.

Quote

Some people dream of success,
while other people get up
every morning and
make it happen

WAYNE HUIZENGA

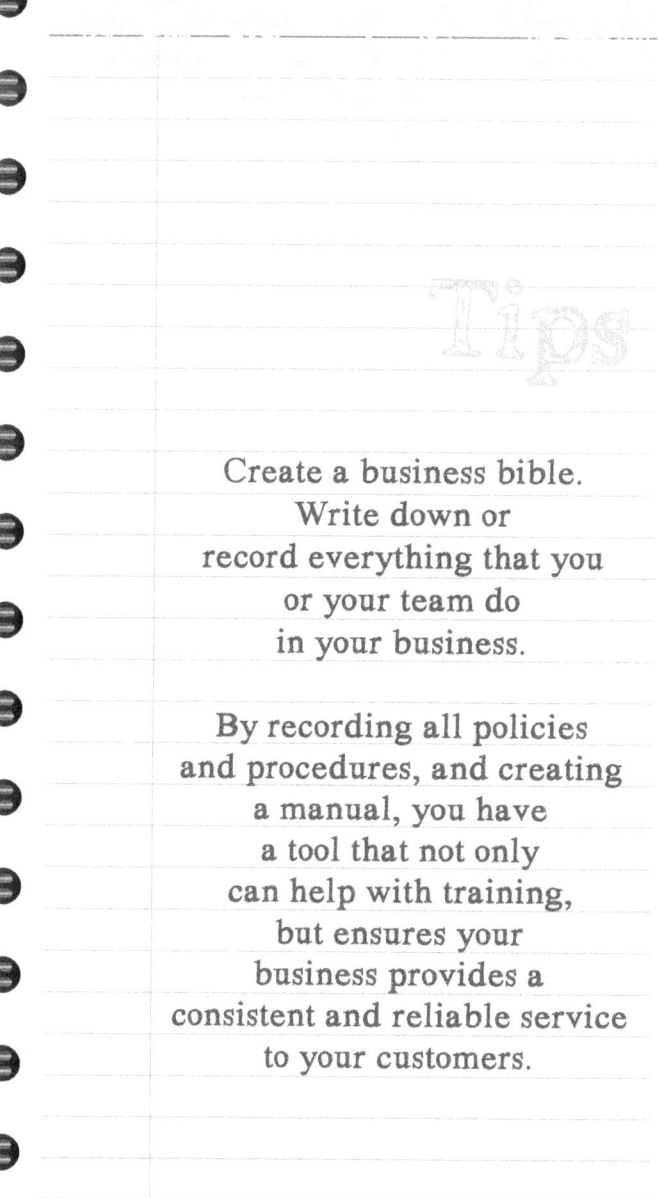

Tips

Create a business bible.
Write down or
record everything that you
or your team do
in your business.

By recording all policies
and procedures, and creating
a manual, you have
a tool that not only
can help with training,
but ensures your
business provides a
consistent and reliable service
to your customers.

Rachel is a mum, entrepreneur, author, and advocate for small businesses. With over 20 years working in admin in a range of industries, she uses her knowledge to help small business grow to their full potential.